Contents

In their own words
Look for these boxes to find inspirational quotes from the kids featured in this book and other famous people who made a difference.

Kids who made a difference

These boxes tell you stories about kids who have done great things to make the world a better place, both now and in the past.

Top tips

Search for these boxes for quick facts about how you can make a difference.

Some words in the book are in bold, **like this**. You can find out what they mean by looking in the glossary.

Why save the environment?

Earth is an amazing place. It is the only planet we know of that supports life. However, our actions are harming it. We face many environmental problems, from air **pollution** to the melting of the ice at the North and South Poles. Luckily, there are young people all over the world who have decided to take the future of the planet into their own hands. They are determined to do something about environmental problems before it is too late.

Earth is sometimes called "the blue planet" because around 70 per cent of it is covered with life-giving water.

Step by step

You might wonder how any young person can make a difference to the problems of a whole planet. Many young people begin with making one small change ... then another ... and another. Several small changes can add up to make a big difference. Other young people find a way to have a huge impact all at once.

Kids who made a difference

In 1985, an eight-year-old Mexican boy, Omar Castillo Gallegos, protested against the destruction of the Chiapas **rainforest** by walking with his father from Mexico City to the town of Chiapas. The walk was nearly 1,300 kilometres (800 miles) long, and it took him 39 days. Once back home, he pitched a tent outside the president's palace until the president finally agreed to meet with him. The president decided to pass laws to protect the Chiapas rainforest.

By destroying rainforests, humans have wiped out many useful animal and plant **species**. Much of Mexico's rainforest is being cleared for cattle ranching.

Going it alone

To make a difference you could watch less television every day. You will use less electricity. Make sure you turn off lights, televisions, and computers when you leave a room. And save water by always turning off the tap when you brush your teeth. What other small changes can you think of?

Working together

In 2008, 16-year-old Sarah Jo Lambert gathered adults, youth groups, and local companies to build an environmental centre in West Texas, USA, called the Lorax Lodge. This was a place where kids could learn how to protect the planet and become strong future leaders. Everything used to create the building was made from **recycled** materials.

Imagine what you could achieve if you teamed up with other kids. You could join a clean-up of litter in a local area. You could suggest making a wildlife garden at school. You could take part in a table-top sale to raise money for a **conservation** organization. The planet-saving possibilities are endless.

Kids who made a difference

Many people use plastic bags to scoop their dog's poop. However, plastic bags stay as litter for many years. In 2000, a 12-year-old Japanese girl called Haruka Maruno thought of a better idea. Haruka designed a poop scoop made from an empty milk carton, which would break down to nothing when it was thrown away. She won a competition and was featured in *Time* magazine as a Hero for the Planet.

In the United Kingdom and United States, the rubbish each person makes in a year weighs the same as a small elephant.

Felix Finkbeiner: planting for the planet

Trees are vital to life on this planet. Trees make **oxygen** for us to breathe, they clean the air and soil, they stop soil being blown away by the wind, and their roots keep water from draining away from the earth. Nearly 40 million square kilometres (15.5 million square miles) of forest cover Earth's surface.

However, vast areas of forest are being cleared. Each year, Earth loses an area of forest the size of Scotland. People cut down the trees to sell the timber, and to build huge ranches and mines. Some types of forest, such as rainforest, are disappearing faster than others.

Ancient forests in Europe are home to rare plants and animals.

Combating climate change

Many scientists think the loss of so many trees has played a big part in changing Earth's weather patterns. There are fewer trees to clean the air and this has heated up the planet. Ice around the North and South Poles has been melting, raising sea levels. In hot, dry areas there has been less rain, while in other areas there have been many big storms, causing flooding and hurricane damage. These are the frightening facts that in 2007 inspired a young German boy, Felix Finkbeiner, to act.

Felix is an ordinary boy with a passion to save Earth's forests.

In their own words

The US President Barack Obama once said, "All across the world, in every kind of environment and region known to man, [there are] increasingly dangerous weather patterns and devastating storms ... [**Climate change**] is real, it's here, and its effects are giving rise to ... the man-made natural disaster."

The Green Belt Movement

One weekend when Felix was just nine, he was preparing for a school presentation, finding out about climate change. Researching on the internet, he came across the story of Wangari Maathai. Wangari was the daughter of farmworkers in Kenya. She saw how difficult it was for farmers to grow crops because of soil blowing away. When Wangari grew up, she tried to stop this problem with a campaign to plant trees. By 2004, her efforts had inspired the planting of over 40 million trees and she won the **Nobel Peace Prize**. Felix wondered why, if Wangari Maathai could have such an impact on tree-planting, why shouldn't he, too?

Felix lives in the town of Pocking, near Munich in Germany.

The first tree Felix planted was a crab apple, like this one.

Stirring up a storm

Felix based his school presentation around a simple but strong idea: "plant for the planet". He aimed to get one million young people in every country to plant a tree each. Felix's classmates thought it was a brilliant idea. Then Felix's teacher asked him to give the same presentation in front of the school's student council and his headteacher. They were excited, too.

Just over two months later, Felix planted his first sapling. News of his Plant for the Planet campaign spread and Felix began giving his presentation to other schools. More students wanted to join in and some offered to help Felix build a website. Suddenly, young people all over Germany were planting trees.

In their own words

Wangari Maathai was a Kenyan environmental campaigner. She said, "It's the little things citizens do. That's what will make the difference. My little thing is planting trees."

Going global

Next, Felix approached the car company Toyota with his idea. He inspired them to **donate** money and the head of Toyota Germany invited Felix to talk at a conference of car dealers, who went away to plant trees, too. In April 2008, 10-year-old Felix called a press meeting to announce that 50,000 new trees had been planted in Germany!

News of Felix's campaign spread around the world. In June 2008, he was on the junior board of the United Nations Environment Programme. He was one of just 10 children in the world chosen to discuss environment-saving ideas to attract young people across the planet. That November, Felix gave a presentation at the **European Parliament**. He invited other nations to start their own Plant for the Planet groups.

In 2008, Felix (right) spoke at the United Nation's Children's Conference in Norway.

Top tips

If you don't have space to plant a tree, ask if you can plant one somewhere else – in a neighbour's garden, or at your school. Some small trees, such as lemon trees, are happy to grow in pots indoors.

The guardians of the globe

By 2011, Felix's organization was running in 131 countries! It had 12 staff and the support of many companies as well as millions of young people. Felix has opened Plant for the Planet academies in countries including China, where children teach others to be **ambassadors**. Felix has said: "We children [have] understood we cannot trust that adults alone will save our future. We have to take our future in our own hands."

In their own words

"A nation that destroys its soils destroys itself. Forests are the lungs of our land, purifying the air and giving fresh strength to our people."

Franklin D Roosevelt, President of the United States from 1933 to 1945

To learn more about Felix's project, visit the website at www.plant-for-the-planet.org/en.

Bindi Irwin: wildlife warrior

Every year, some plants and animals disappear forever because humans destroy their **habitats**. Animals currently in danger include mountain gorillas, leatherback sea turtles, and Sumatran tigers.

Many organizations work to save wildlife from extinction (dying out completely), including zoos. In the past, zoos were criticized for keeping unhappy animals in unnatural conditions, just to make money. However, today most zoos are run by experts, who look after the animals well. Modern zoos educate people about animal conservation. They use their money to support breeding programmes around the world. One such place is Australia Zoo, run by the family of a girl called Bindi Irwin.

Young Bindi Irwin with her father, Steve, and her mother, Terri.

A family cause

Bindi Irwin was born in 1998 into a family committed to helping animals. Her grandparents had set up a wildlife park that rescued **endangered** crocodiles, snakes, and kangaroos. Her mother, Terri, had set up a rescue centre for injured animals, before she met Bindi's father, Steve. Steve Irwin was known as TV's "Crocodile Hunter".

Steve made TV programmes in which he searched out and rescued endangered reptiles. Terri and Bindi flew with him around the world to film. Steve developed his parents' wildlife park into Australia Zoo and, in 2002, he and Terri set up the Wildlife Warriors foundation to fund conservation projects. Bindi wanted to help, but she was just four years old.

Top tips

You can tell that a zoo cares for animals if:

- **enclosures** are like the animals' natural environments
- animals have space to run or fly
- animals have interesting things to do
- it supports animal breeding or conservation projects.

Bindi's home, Australia Zoo, is near Beerwah, in Queensland, Australia.

Life at the zoo

Bindi began by helping at the zoo. She learned about the animals there and took on daily chores to look after them. As well as learning about all the animals' habits, Bindi became responsible for checking on the zoo's giant Galapagos land tortoise every day and for counting all the shingleback skinks (type of lizard found in Australia). She enjoyed feeding and caring for the dangerous animals, such as crocodiles and snakes. However, Bindi wanted to do more to help endangered animals.

Top tips

Not everyone is able to look after animals at a zoo, but you can still help the zoos' work. Instead of a birthday present, why not ask someone to pay for you to "adopt" a zoo animal? If you would like to get involved in caring for animals that need your help, ask if you can volunteer at an animal rescue shelter. These places often depend on volunteers.

Kid power

Bindi was already well known because of her famous dad, and she wanted to reach out to other young people. The Irwins came up with the idea of creating a clothing line modelled by Bindi and her brother, Robert. This would raise money that they could use to help the zoo and its Wildlife Warrior projects.

As Bindi neared six years old, she also thought she could use her birthday to help promote the zoo's conservation work. The Irwins celebrated that day by allowing all kids into the zoo for free. They hoped that the visitors would learn about the importance of conservation.

Bindi befriended Australia Zoo's Galapagos land tortoise, Harriet, who is over 170 years old.

To learn more about the Irwins' Wildlife Warriors charity, visit the website at wildlifewarriors.org.au.

Fun fundraising

Bindi’s parents had always donated money from Steve's popular television programmes to the zoo and its conservation projects. Bindi wanted to do the same, by making films for children. She made two DVDs of exercise routines for kids that were inspired by animals, a television series called *Bindi the Jungle Girl*, and a recording of fun jungle songs called *Trouble in the Jungle*. She hoped that making these would encourage kids to focus on wildlife and conservation. Soon Bindi was donating her earnings to the zoo and its conservation projects, just like her parents.

Bindi has loved animals from a very young age.

Kids who made a difference

Nine-year-old Amy Jones, from Warwickshire in the UK, has written three stories about dolphins. She hopes they will spread the word about the dangers that dolphins face in the wild. Amy is giving all the proceeds from the sale of her books to the Marine Conservation Society. Amy says, "You don't need to live at a zoo to help animals."

Tragedy strikes

Life for the Irwins and the wildlife they cared for seemed to be going well. Bindi had been working very hard on her DVDs to raise awareness about the importance of wildlife conservation. However, before Bindi's work could be released, tragedy struck. Her father was killed in September 2006 by a **stingray** while he was filming in the ocean off the Australian coast. Bindi was just eight years old. The whole family was terribly upset and the future of the zoo and its conservation projects seemed to be at risk. Nobody could have blamed Bindi if she had suddenly begun to hate animals and want nothing to do with them. So what did she do?

In their own words

Bindi's dad, the conservationist Steve Irwin, once said "I have no fear of losing my life – if I have to save a koala or a crocodile or a kangaroo or a snake, mate, I will save it . . . Born a Wildlife Warrior, die a Wildlife Warrior."

Staying strong

Bindi became even more determined to work for animal conservation. She gave a moving and inspirational speech at her father's memorial service, which was broadcast to millions on Australian TV. She gave the go-ahead for her movies and television show to be released. Then she began touring around the world, appearing on talk shows to explain how she wanted to continue her father's work, educating people about endangered species and helping animals.

In their own words

Bindi has this to say about conservation: "Every time we lose an animal species, it's like losing a brick from the house. Pretty soon, the house just falls down."

The orangutan is one of the animals that the Wildlife Warriors fund helps protect.

Bindi the Wildlife Warrior

On Bindi's ninth birthday in 2007, she became an official staff member at Australia Zoo. Soon afterwards, she starred in *Free Willy: Escape from Pirate's Cove*, a film about ocean conservation. At the age of twelve, Bindi began writing storybooks, inspired by her life at the zoo, to spread the word to more kids about conservation. Bindi wants to go on to even bigger and more important projects as she gets older.

Top tips

If you would like to get involved in animal conservation, you could support one of the animals helped by the Wildlife Warriors foundation. These include Asian elephants in Cambodia, tigers and orangutans in Indonesia, black rhinoceros in Kenya, and cheetahs in South Africa.

Free Willy: Escape from Pirate's Cove tells the story of Kirra (played by Bindi) who rescues a stranded baby orca whale.

Tom Youngman: a greener vision

We all have a carbon footprint. This is a measure of how much **carbon dioxide** we produce in our daily activities, such as using a computer, wearing clothes, or driving a car. Carbon dioxide is one of the main **greenhouse gases**. These are gases produced by burning coal or oil for fuel. They harm the environment by warming up the planet, causing climate change.

If we do not reduce our carbon footprints, there may be terrible results in the future. The polar ice caps will melt and sea levels will rise, causing flooding. Some regions will become wetter, having more storms and hurricanes, while other regions will become hotter and drier. If habitats are damaged, the creatures that live in them could die.

Kids who made a difference

In 2007, 11-year-old Jonny Cohen of Chicago, USA, came up with a simple invention to reduce carbon footprints. He had the idea for a panel made of a light, see-through plastic, called plexiglass, that could fix on to the front of school buses. These "Green Shields" made the buses sleeker, so they used less fuel and reduced the greenhouse gases they created.

Carbon footprint crusader

In 2008, Tom Youngman was a 14-year-old schoolboy from Bath in Somerset, UK. He was passionate about green issues, particularly reducing carbon footprints. But he never dreamed that just three years later he would have made a name for himself as one of the leading young **environmentalists** in the country. So how did he manage it?

Tom Youngman lives in a historic city called Bath in the UK.

Tom Youngman is a schoolboy with great ideas for saving the environment.

Reducing carbon at school

Tom joined the Environmental Action Group at his school, and ended up leading it. He inspired the other members to take part in carbon-footprint-reducing activities. For example, they gave teachers fake "penalty tickets" whenever they left computer monitors and lights on, wasting electricity. The school was awarded a Green Flag by the Eco Schools Initiative in 2011. This is a prize that recognizes a school's contribution to protecting the environment.

Branching out

Tom did not stop there. He sent out letters to environmental groups in other schools in the area, suggesting that they hold regular meetings to see what they could do to reduce carbon in the local community. This created a new group called Green Vision. Tom and other members aim to make Bath and the surrounding area more environmentally friendly and a more pleasant place to live. Their projects have included tending an allotment and running a Youth Climate Conference to discuss new ideas.

It is difficult for a school to win a Green Flag Award, but Tom Youngman has helped King Edward School in Bath win one twice.

Top tips

Tom and his Environmental Action Group reduced their school's carbon footprint by:

- recycling paper, printer cartridges, and mobile phones.
- providing waste paper for note-taking in class.
- setting up a **compost heap** for waste from the school garden.
- getting the school to replace plastic cups with reusable china ones.
- holding a Recycled Fashion Show and Environment Day.

Maybe you could try these ideas at your school, too.

Green Vision often brightens up unloved wasteland.

Getting involved with government

In 2010, Tom joined the government's Youth Advisory Panel on climate change. This gives young people a say in government energy policies. After all, it is young people who will have to live with the consequences of these policies. Tom helped to prepare a report on the options for future energy. His team wanted to persuade the government to use their power to help save the planet!

Winning ways

In March 2011, Tom was nominated for an award as an inspirational young environmentalist. A month later, he represented Britain at the United Nations' climate change negotiations in South Africa. Tom is turning into a very influential young person when it comes to shaping the planet's future.

Kids who made a difference

Ten-year-old Harshit Agrawal from Bangalore, India, started a prize-winning club in 2001. The group of kids from his neighbourhood called themselves the Little Eco Friends. They wanted to stop the use of plastic bags, which harmed animals who got trapped in them or ate them. So they made cloth bags out of old clothes and gave them to shops and people in the street. Harshit also started a Zero Waste programme at his school.

To learn more about Tom's Green Vision group, visit their website at www.greenvisionmovement.org.

Top tips

Here are some things you can do to reduce your carbon footprint:

- If you feel cold, put on an extra jumper instead of asking to have the heating on.
- Walk or ride a bike instead of asking to be driven.
- Carry a reusable bottle instead of buying plastic bottles of water.
- Look for secondhand clothes and toys instead of buying new ones, and borrow books and DVDs from the library.
- Grow some of your own food in your garden or in pots on your windowsill.

Growing your own food reduces the carbon dioxide made by food manufacturers in transporting their supplies to the shops.

Adeline Suwana: saving Indonesia

Countries in Southeast Asia have already begun to see the impact of **global warming** and climate change. In recent years, the weather has become more extreme, with frequent heatwaves causing **droughts** in some regions. In other places, violent storms called typhoons and cyclones are causing floods more and more often. In 2009, the Asian Development Bank published a regional review of climate change and found that Indonesia was one of the countries worst affected.

The capital city of Indonesia, Jakarta, is flooded every year. Often, more than half the city disappears under water.

In their own words

Ira Wanoni was an Indonesian flood victim in 2010: "I heard a roar and suddenly the river near my home broke its banks. Water mixed with rocks, mud, and logs gushed out. Many people didn't have time to save themselves."

Fighting the floods

In 2008, 12-year-old Adeline Suwana experienced flooding first hand in her home in Jakarta. She and her family had to move out of their home because there was no electricity and clean water.

Adeline did some research into the cause of the flooding and began finding out about climate change. She quickly realized that it wasn't just humans paying the price, but the environment was suffering, too. She became determined to do something about it.

Adeline Suwana lives in Indonesia's capital city, Jakarta.

A mission for mangroves

Adeline read that mangrove trees are important to hold back floods caused by rising seawater. Mangrove trees grow in forests between the land and sea. They are muddy, swampy places filled with mosquitoes, snakes, and spiders. However, the trees act as barriers for wind and waves. They keep soil in place and stop water washing onto the land. During floods, their roots help to soak up extra water, too.

Adeline discovered that mangrove swamps are some of the world's most threatened forests. People chop them down to sell the timber, or to clear the land for farming or building. Mangrove swamps were disappearing from Indonesia at an alarming rate. Adeline decided she could not sit by and let this happen.

Adeline Suwana and her friends are fighting the destruction of mangrove swamps in Indonesia.

Getting organized

During the school summer holiday, Adeline invited 150 classmates and other friends to plant 200 mangrove trees along the coastline in a nature park. The teenagers learned how Indonesia has almost one quarter of all the world's mangrove forest. They realized how important mangroves were to protect Indonesia from the sea, and how many fish, birds, and reptiles relied on them to survive.

But Adeline did not stop there. Next, she formed a group called Sahabat Alam (Friends of Nature) with her 150 supporters, to continue her environmental work. Adeline wanted to raise awareness and educate many more young people about the importance of Indonesian wildlife, and encourage them to protect nature in all sorts of ways.

Kids who made a difference

Seventeen-year-old Amy Beal said she lived in "the driest state in the driest country in the world": Adelaide, in Australia. The main source of water was the Murray River, but it was drying up through overuse, and wildlife there was dying. Amy organized a conference to educate young people about the problem. Because she and others spoke out, in 2003 the Australian government announced an improvement programme for the Murray River.

To learn more about Sahabat Alam, visit their website at www.sahabat-alam.com/en.

Saving the seas

Adeline and Sahabat Alam learned about a conservation area for hawksbill turtles and the importance of protecting their ocean habitat. They launched a campaign to stop people throwing rubbish into seas and rivers. The group also visited the island of Pulau Pramuka, where the **coral reef** has been damaged. They helped to plant new coral, to provide homes for many types of sea creature.

Corals are clusters of tiny animals with their skeletons outside their bodies. They provide a home for 25 per cent of all ocean creatures.

Adeline also joined an environmental clean-up after flooding from a collapsed **dam** resulted in many deaths. She and her friends began using bicycles instead of travelling in cars, to reduce pollution. The group also set up a scheme where **clean energy** from a waterfall provides electricity to villages.

Spreading the word

Adeline has tried to reach out through Sahabat Alam to as many people as possible. She has presented her ideas to schools, cooperated with government agencies, created a website, recorded a song, and is producing a television programme. She has won many important awards and represented Indonesia in the 2010 Children and Youth International Conference "Let's Take Care of the Planet", in Brazil. She aims to inspire young people all over the planet to take saving the world into their own hands, and she has said that she will never stop!

Adeline reaches out to as many people as she can.

Top tips

If you would like to get involved in conservation work, why not join a Scouts or Girl Guides group and persuade them to set up projects where you live?

Alexander Zerphy: horseshoe crab hero

In 2007, 10-year-old Alexander Zerphy of Maryland, USA, was digging in the sand at his local beach. As he dug, he spotted some small clear balls with tiny creatures swimming inside. He had never seen them before, but when he did some research he discovered that they were eggs! The tiny creatures he could see inside the eggs were the young of the Atlantic horseshoe crab. These unusual creatures are not actually crabs, but are more closely related to spiders and scorpions. They have lived on the earth for at least 450 million years. Horseshoe crabs were here even before the dinosaurs!

A baby horseshoe crab. A female can lay 60,000 to 120,000 eggs. But many shore birds eat the eggs before they hatch.

Critical creatures

Scientists have discovered that the blood of horseshoe crabs contains a substance known as LAL. This substance can be used to detect harmful **bacteria** on medical equipment and in drugs, saving countless lives. This makes horseshoe crabs very important to humans. They are also very important to shorebirds. The crabs are their main source of food.

However, horseshoe crabs are in danger of dying out. Humans are damaging their habitats by building on beaches and shorelines. When Alex learned this, he became determined to help protect them.

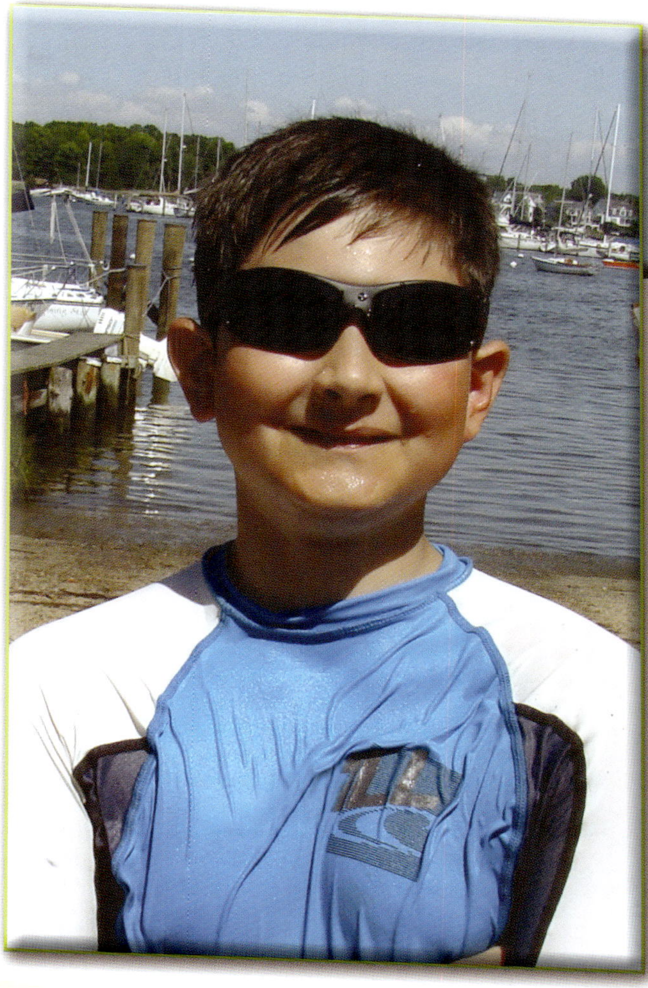

Alexander Zerphy has become a passionate protector of horseshoe crabs.

In their own words

The nature journalist Alex Reshanov says that the horseshoe crab has "survived changes to the planet that killed off countless other creatures".

Spreading the word

The following year, Alex entered a national contest to improve the life of an animal. He wrote an essay and created an awareness campaign with a logo and information cards for "Planet Horseshoe Crab". He got through to the final of the competition! Next, eleven-year-old Alex applied for an Aquatic Research Education **grant**, which would help him do research into horseshoe crabs.

Alex got his whole family involved in his research. His parents examined breeding horseshoe crabs at their local beach. Alex also began keeping his own horseshoe crabs through a scheme called the Raising Horseshoe Crabs in the Classroom Project. This project provides equipment and information to schools so students can keep horseshoe crabs and learn about how important they are.

In their own words

Alexander Zerphy says, "We are all connected! ... Horseshoe crabs save human lives every day; this project is dedicated to returning the favour."

Making his mark

Alex set his sights high, and by the autumn of 2008 he had managed to set up a site for his research, called the Chesapeake Conservation Center. It was named after Chesapeake Bay, where he had first found the horseshoe crabs. He created horseshoe crab information cards and T-shirts to raise people's awareness. In 2009, Alex went further by asking to meet the local mayor to discuss the importance of horseshoe crabs. The mayor was so impressed with Alex's efforts that she had two information boards set up locally.

Here. Alex is shown with the mayor and one of his new horseshoe crab information boards.

To learn more about Alex's conservation centre, visit the website at www.cc-center.org.

Educating others

Alex's efforts to help save horseshoe crabs were so impressive that the Annapolis Maritime Museum invited him to teach other schoolchildren about the creatures. Following this, Alex developed a proper Planet Horseshoe Crab **curriculum** for kids to study! In addition, Alex organized a Naturalist Club to try to improve people's knowledge about nature in general. He became the student advisor for The **Terrapin** Institute, which works to protect the beach homes that are vital to the survival of terrapins and other species, as well as horseshoe crabs.

Alexander Zerphy's local beach is one of the world's most important habitats for horseshoe crabs.

An eco hero – it's official!

At the age of 13, Alex won first place in a worldwide award scheme – he was named the Action for Nature International Eco Hero 2010. Now millions of people across the world would hear of the plight of horseshoe crabs – a local issue for Alex, but one that affects the well-being of the whole planet.

Alex Zerphy's work has led to him being officially recognized as an international eco hero.

Kids who made a difference

In 2001, nine-year-old Henry Cilley, from Chicago, USA, found out about some building work that was going to take place near his school. The endangered Blanding's turtle lived in a nature reserve nearby, and Henry worried that this development would put the turtles at risk. He gave speeches to local groups, got 700 people to sign a **petition**, and protested to all the groups involved in the plans. The building company agreed to protect the turtles!

You can make a difference

When there is a problem it is easy to leave other people to deal with it. If we all take that approach to environmental issues, Earth and all the life on it faces a very bleak future. The good news is that it's not too late. And everyone can make a difference.

You can make a difference close to home by picking up litter.

Don't delay, start today

The stories in this book show that when it comes to saving the planet, it doesn't matter how young you are. If you would like to protect the environment, think about which concerns are closest to your heart. Start small – little things can make a big difference if enough people do them. Be positive and enthusiastic and get others to help. Most important of all, begin now and don't give up!

Kids who made a difference

In 1990 in Japan, Aika Tsubota produced a comic book about caring for the environment, called *Secrets of the Earth*. Unfortunately, soon afterwards, she died. Her parents printed copies for her schoolmates. News of Aika's story spread through Japan and it was made into a textbook. It has also been translated into many different languages and displayed at the United Nations' headquarters in New York.

In their own words

Japanese schoolgirl Aika Tsubota gave this advice: "The most important thing is for people to stop feeling powerless because they are only one person. You can make a difference! If everybody pitches in, I know we can turn this planet into a beautiful place."

If one person makes a change, their behaviour can spread outwards like a ripple, affecting many others.

Making a difference map

Arctic Ocean
Tom Youngman (pages 22–27) organizes student environmental groups in Bath, England.
Haruka Maruno (page 6) invented an eco-friendly poop scoop in Japan.
Felix Finkbeiner (pages 8–13) started his tree-planting campaign in his home town of Pocking, Germany.
ASIA
EUROPE
Harshit Agrawal (page 26) started an environmental group in Bangalore, India.
Pacific Ocean
AFRICA
Adeline Suwana (pages 28–33) works to protect wildlife from her home in Jakarta, Indonesia.
AUSTRALASIA
Indian Ocean
Amy Beal (page 31) worked to protect the Murray River in South Australia.
Wangari Maathai (pages 10–11) began a tree-planting project in Nairobi, Kenya.
Bindi Irwin (pages 14–21) helps her family at Australia Zoo in Queensland, Australia.
Southern Ocean
ANTARCTICA

Tips on making a difference

Most environmental experts would agree that the number one way people can help to save the environment is to reduce their carbon footprint. This is because the lifestyle changes you can make to reduce your carbon footprint will not just have the effect of fighting climate change. They can help the environment in a wide range of ways. Here are some steps you can take:

The first step is to work out what your carbon footprint is. There are websites which can help you to do this, such as **www.cooltheworld.com/kidscarboncalculator.php**. Websites like this will also give you tips on the lifestyle changes you can make to reduce your carbon footprint.

The changes you make will not just have the effect of fighting climate change. They can help the environment in a wide range of ways. Making simple changes in your daily habits can help save energy and water, reduce waste and pollution, and preserve resources and habitats.

Volunteering and fundraising

Another great way to help save the planet is to volunteer to help a good environmental cause. You could help in lots of ways, from offering hands-on help at litter-pick-up day, to holding a table-top sale to raise money for an environmental project. By volunteering, you can not only help the environment, you can also make new friends, learn new skills, and have fun!

Choosing a charity

It's important to research a charity before you donate your money or time. An adult can help you do this. Here are some tips:

* First, find a charity that helps a cause you are interested in. Websites such as www.guidestar.org.uk and www.charitychoice.co.uk allow you to search charities by topic.
* Find out how the charity uses its money. Does most of it go to the people who need it? There are websites listed on page 47 that can help you find out.
* Once you've chosen a charity, find out what help they need. Some are looking for volunteers, others for donations of money or goods.

Starting your own project

If you can't find the right project, you might want to start your own. This can be a big job, so don't be afraid to ask for help! Learn as much as you can about the problem you want to solve. Is there anyone else working towards the same goals, either in your community or elsewhere? You might be able to learn from them, or even get their support. Once you decide on a particular project, develop a plan to reach your goal.

Talk with a trusted adult

Many of the young people featured in this book had help and support from their parents and other trusted adults. You should discuss your idea with a parent, teacher, or club leader. An adult can provide advice and help you stay safe.

Glossary

ambassador someone who teaches others about a cause and sets an example by helping the cause

bacteria germs that cause illnesses

carbon dioxide gas that we can neither see nor smell

clean energy sources of energy that are thought to be environmentally-friendly, such as energy made from the wind and waves, or the Sun

climate change long-term change in Earth's weather and temperature

compost heap pile of natural waste materials, such as leaves and vegetables, that are left to rot

conservation activities which protect animals or environments that are in danger

coral reef mound or ridge under the sea, which is made of tiny living animals called coral

curriculum plan for study

dam structure built to hold water back

donate give as a gift, to help a person or project

drought long period of very dry weather that creates problems for living things that need water

enclosure area that is contained by a fence, wall, or netting

endangered animal or habitat that is at risk of dying out

environmentalist person who works to protect the natural environment

European Parliament group of people who make laws for all the countries in Europe

global warming gradual warming of the Earth's atmosphere caused mainly by gases released when we burn fuels

grant gift of money

greenhouse gases gases in the air that are increasing due to human activities, such as cutting down forests and burning coal and oil. These increased amounts are causing the climate to change all around the planet.

habitat natural area in which a creature or plant lives

Nobel Peace Prize important prize that is given once every year to the person who has done most in the world to help people live in harmony

oxygen gas that we can neither see nor smell, but which we need to breathe

petition protest that collects as many people's signatures as possible in support of a cause

pollution chemicals, such as car exhaust fumes, or energy, such as noise or light, that are harmful to the environment

rainforest forests in hot areas which regularly have heavy rainfall

recycle treat or process materials so that they can be used again

species type of animal or plant

stingray flat fish, related to sharks, which has a sting in its long tail

terrapin type of turtle that lives in the eastern and southern United States

Find out more

Books

101 Ways to Save the Planet, Deborah Underwood (Raintree, 2011)

Climate Change (Planet Under Pressure), Mike Unwin (Raintree, 2007)

Endangered Animals (100 Facts), Steve Parker (Miles Kelly, 2010)

Why Should I Switch Off the Light? (One Small Step), MJ Knight (Franklin Watts, 2008)

Websites

www.recyclezone.org.uk
A website that will give you ideas for how you can reduce, reuse, and recycle.

www.meetthegreens.org
A US-based site where you can follow the adventures of a cartoon family who are trying to be environmentally conscious.

kids.nationalgeographic.co.uk/kids
Quizzes, videos, games, and tips to bring you closer to nature and the world's creatures.

www.kidsrgreen.org/krg.html
Tips and advice for kids who want to go green at home and in school.

www.charity-commission.gov.uk
The Charity Commission regulates charities in the UK. Visit their website to find information on charities and their projects, and to learn about setting up your own.

www.charitychoice.co.uk
Here you can search for charities by name or by category.

www.junction49.co.uk
This is an online forum for young people to share ideas about helping others.

Index